LITTLE WONDERS

THE WONDER OF
Little
GIRLS

Phyllis Hobe

The C.R. Gibson Company
Norwalk, Connecticut 06856

LITTLE WONDERS

The Wonder of Mom
The Wonder of Dad
The Wonder of Friends
The Wonder of Babies
The Wonder of Little Girls
The Wonder of Little Boys

Published by The C.R. Gibson Company,
Norwalk, Connecticut 06856

Printed in the U.S.A.
Designed by Deborah Michel

ISBN 0-8378-8327-X
GB406

When a little girl
says, "I love you,"
it's impossible to find
anything wrong with
the world.

One of the
proudest moments in
a little girl's life is when
she learns to tie her
own shoelaces.

It's hard for little girls to finish telling a joke because they can't wait till the end to start laughing.

A little girl
dancing around the
living room is like a
ballerina—
until she crashes
into a chair.

Little girls love
to open presents—
even though they always
know ahead of time
what's in them.

A little girl
loves to show you the
gap where her tooth
used to be.

Once a little
girl learns to write,
you can expect to find
letters addressed
to you all over
the house.

*L*ittle girls like
to do things their
way, even if it takes
twice as long.

Before you read a new bedtime story to a little girl, she'll want to know if it has a happy ending... If it doesn't, you'd better invent one in a hurry.

It takes a little
girl a long time to say
her prayers because she
doesn't want anybody
to go without
a blessing.

A little girl dressed up in her mother's clothes is a preview of coming attractions.

Little girls love
to tell secrets—but
only if you promise
not to tell.

The sight of
little girls selling
lemonade can bring
traffic to a halt.

Stubbornness
in action: A little girl
building a sand castle as
the waves roll in.

Very few things
in life hurt as much
as a little girl's
skinned knee.

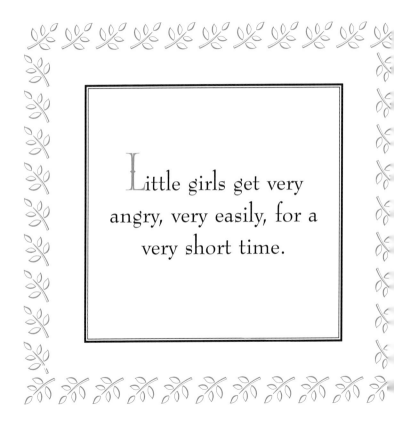

Little girls get very
angry, very easily, for a
very short time.

Why is it that when you take a little girl with you on your shopping trip, you somehow always end up in a fitting room with an armful of clothes in her size?

It's hard to believe that a little girl with a ponytail and pink nail polish could steal second base and spit the dust out of her mouth and it's even harder to believe that you cheered wildly when she did it.

Little girls don't like:
big brothers,
little brothers,
or anybody's brothers.

*L*ittle girls like:
movie stars,
teachers,
and one boy in
their class.

Little girls
can turn an
allowance into high
finance.

Give a little girl a
piggy bank and you'll
see that she knows a lot
more about money than
how to spend it.

$\mathcal{L}$ ittle girls
are very good at
telling the truth—
as they see it.

You'll know a
little girl is growing up
when she wants to fix
her own hair, when she
says she'll read to you
at bedtime, when she

doesn't want you to
hold her hand crossing
the street, and doesn't
want you to come into
her room—except
during thunderstorms.

A little girl
can be so brave
when she gets her
shots that everyone
else cries.

A little girl who goes to a supermarket with her father comes home with everything her mother would never buy.

*W*hen little girls
ask you a question,
be sure to answer them
truthfully because
they'll believe every
word you say.

*L*ittle girls aren't
afraid of the dark—
it's their dolls who
like to sleep with the
lights on.

The shortest
route to a temper
tantrum is to tell a
little girl to wear
something she
doesn't like.

The only friends
little girls make are
best friends.

If you think little girls can't set goals and reach them, watch a little girl learn to ride a bike.

Every little girl needs
a place where she can
keep things she doesn't
want anyone to see—
even if she forgets why
she put them there.

A little girl may
be very possessive with
her dolls, but she'll give
all of them to a little
girl who has none.

Little girls play
by the rules, the
trouble comes when
they can't agree what
the rules are.

There is
absolutely no limit
to the amount of
ice cream little
girls can eat.

*W*hen little girls
don't want to do
what you tell them
to do, their silence
speaks volumes.

*B*y the time you figure out a little girl's favorite foods, she doesn't like them anymore.

The lights dim,
the curtains part, and there
she is—your little girl,
second from the left
fourth row from the front...
anyone can see she's a star!

$\mathcal{A}$ little girl
can tell you she loves
you without saying a
word... just by wanting
to be with you.

A little girl who
helps out in the kitchen
is pure delight—
if you have time to
clean up after her.

When a little
girl is sick, she may
not ask you to stay
home from work, but
she's awfully glad
when you do.

A little girl's hug
can make a grandparent
forget all the rules.

Seeing your
little girl in school
makes you realize that
she's not so little.

When a little girl sleeps over at a friend's house for the first time, her parents don't sleep at all.

Taking a little
girl to work with you
for a day makes both of
you feel important.

Heads of state could learn a few things about diplomacy from a little girl deciding who will get invited to her birthday party.

If you tell a little
girl to do something,
she may not—
if you ask for her
help, she'll do anything
you want.

There isn't
a nicer gift than a
little girl bringing you
breakfast in bed.

When a little
girl builds a snowman,
she'll get up several
times at night to see
if it's melting.

It's worth getting
sick just to have a little
girl play nurse.

*There is nothing
that can restore you to
happiness faster than a little
girl's arms around
your neck.*

Let a little girl
help you plant seeds
in your garden, and
Spring will be the most
exciting season you've
ever known.

The first day of school for
a little girl is an adventure—
for her parents it's a tug at
the heart. She feels grownup...
they know she soon
will be.